STUDY GUIDE

A Survey of Church History

Part 4, AD 1600–1800

W. Robert Godfrey

LIGONIER MINISTRIES

Renew your Mind.

LIGONIER.ORG | 800-435-4343

Introduction

As the Protestant church carried the Reformation into the seventeenth and eighteenth centuries, it faced numerous challenges from without and from within. Europe was witnessing dramatic changes as the medieval world began to give way to the modern. Having broken with the Roman Catholic Church, Protestants faced the prospect of ever-deepening division among its own members. But despite the numerous threats, the Reformed church pressed forward. In this series, join Dr. Robert Godfrey as he surveys the history of the Reformed church in the English-speaking world. You will study the Puritans from England to New England. You will also meet such notable figures as John and Charles Wesley, George Whitefield, and Jonathan Edwards, all of whom played major roles in the First Great Awakening.

1

Continuing the Reformation

MESSAGE INTRODUCTION

The Reformation was a turning point in the history of the church. And in its aftermath, Protestants wanted to continue along the trajectory set by the Reformers. They sought to further develop a theology which was reformed according to Scripture, and to continue to purify, discipline, and grow the church. Accordingly, there were many internal challenges facing the fledgling Reformed church. And in addition to these internal challenges, there were many external challenges. In this lesson, Dr. Godfrey will explain the major challenges that faced the Reformed church as it sought to be a faithful witness in an ever-changing world.

SCRIPTURE READINGS

Matthew 28:16–20; Romans 13:1–7

TEACHING OBJECTIVES

1. To explore the numerous challenges that faced the church after the Reformation
2. To examine how the divisions within the church changed how believers saw one another
3. To see that the fracturing of the church left Western culture without a unifying cultural force

QUOTATION

Protestantism . . . associates the unity of the church first of all with the oneness of the head of the church, with the communion of all believers through one and the same Spirit, with Christ and with each other, and further, with the unity of faith, hope, and love, and of baptism, and so forth. This unity, though primarily spiritual in character, nevertheless exists objectively and really, and it does not remain completely invisible. It manifests itself outwardly—albeit in a very imperfect way—and at least to some degree comes to light in that which all Christian churches have in common. No Christianity exists above or beneath religious differences, but there is indeed a Christianity present amid religious differences. Because we tend to be most aware of the differences and schisms in Christianity, we constantly run the danger of disregarding this—nevertheless truly existing—unity. That which unites all true Christians is always more than that which separates them.

—Herman Bavinck

LECTURE OUTLINE

I. Introduction
- A. This series will examine the development of the Reformed church in the seventeenth and eighteenth centuries.
- B. It is a period of expanding diversity—theologically, geographically, and culturally.

II. Continuing the Reformation
- A. The Reformed church sought to take the foundation laid by the Reformers and continue to build on it.
- B. In a quickly changing world, the church faced numerous challenges.

III. Geographical Challenges
- A. Most Europeans did not understand how vast the world really was.
- B. With European expansion into the Americas, Africa, and Asia, it became clear how many people had never heard about Christ.

IV. Political Challenges
- A. By the seventeenth century, individual nations, along with their rulers, grew in importance.
- B. Rulers were limited in power by other nobility and by parliaments.
  - i. A parliament is a gathering of representatives of various peoples from whom a ruler had to get permission.
  - ii. Parliaments had to approve raising taxes and raising armies.
- C. In the seventeenth century, many rulers wanted to get rid of parliaments and rule by divine right, becoming absolute rulers.
- D. This desire for absolute rule created great tension between rulers and other forces in society that wanted to rule a nation.

V. The Challenge of a Divided Church
- A. Until the Reformation, there was essentially one united institutional church.
- B. In addition to the Roman Catholic, Lutheran, and Reformed churches, numerous Anabaptist churches sprang up, as well as other groups.
- C. Most Christians had thought of the church in terms of true or false.

VI. Cultural Challenges
- A. Religion held European culture together from the beginning.
- B. The Roman Catholic Church provided the cultural backbone for the Western world for over a millennium.
- C. With the division of the church, it was difficult to determine what could hold culture together.
- D. Some thought a basic Christianity could fill this role, but increasingly people turned to natural law and human reason as a potential unifying force.

VII. Theological Challenges
- A. Protestants of the late sixteenth and early seventeenth centuries found themselves challenged by renewal in the Roman Catholic Church.
  - i. Earlier Reformers, like Luther and Calvin, were much better educated than leaders within the Roman Catholic Church.
  - ii. The most prominent Roman Catholic theologian who arose was Robert Bellarmine.
    1. He wrote a work called the *Controversies*, which sought to answer Protestant theology.
    2. Answering Bellarmine required Protestants to provide a very technical defense of their faith.
- B. The Reformed church was challenged by a renewed Lutheranism.
- C. A new branch of theology called Socinianism developed.
  - i. It doubted the authority of Scripture.
  - ii. It doubted the divinity of Christ.

STUDY QUESTIONS

1. Dr. Godfrey thinks that the study of church history gets more difficult as it approaches the present because _____.
   - a. There are too many sources to evaluate
   - b. It begins to show extraordinary diversity
   - c. Historians are more biased about the recent past
   - d. Roman Catholics have dominated the writing of church history

2. This series will focus primarily on the Evangelical and Reformed churches.
   - a. True
   - b. False

3. In this lesson, we saw how the church was challenged in all of the following ways, except _____.
   - a. Geographically
   - b. Ethnically
   - c. Politically
   - d. Theologically

4. In the seventeenth century, Europe saw many peaceful transitions from monarchy to democracy.
   a. True
   b. False

5. The most famous Roman Catholic theologian, with whom Protestants had to contend, was _____.
   a. Ignatius of Loyola
   b. Robert Bellarmine
   c. Francis Turretin
   d. Casper Olevianus

DISCUSSION QUESTIONS

1. With the church's growing understanding of the size of the world, its concern for and participation in missions grew. How should our growing knowledge of other parts of the world, and the ease with which it's learned, inform and impassion our prayers for those who have still not yet heard the gospel?

2. Formalism was a major concern for the Puritans. Have you ever found yourself simply going through the motions, whether at church or with the spiritual disciplines, without engaging your mind and affections? What are some ways to combat this tendency?

3. Following the Reformation, among Protestants there was a shift from thinking of the church in terms of true or false, to a dichotomy of pure/less pure. How can this dichotomy allow churches today to retain their distinctives, while at the same time fostering unity?

4. Christianity was the glue that held European culture together for centuries. This changed with the Enlightenment. What are some modern institutions and cultural practices that stem from a Christian past? Do you think these will persist into the future?

2

Scholastic Theology

MESSAGE INTRODUCTION

One might think of scholastic theology as dry, nitpicky, and irrelevant, but that couldn't be further from the truth. Many scholastic theologians were learned, lively, and deeply concerned not just about orthodoxy, but also piety. Although their writings are often challenging, Christians today can benefit greatly from these past saints. In this lecture, Dr. Godfrey will survey the scholastic movement, pointing out its importance and relevance for the church—past and present.

SCRIPTURE READINGS

Romans 14:1–12; 1 Peter 3:15

TEACHING OBJECTIVES

1. To introduce the style and approach of scholastic theology
2. To explain the need for precision in theology
3. To show how past theologians can benefit the church today

QUOTATION

So far is God from changing his decrees to suit the changes of men, that on the contrary every change of human acts proceeds from the eternal and irrevocable decree of God.

—Francis Turretin

LECTURE OUTLINE

I. Scholasticism

    A. The renewed theology that developed in the early seventeenth century is often described as scholasticism.

    B. Scholasticism is theology as it's done in the schools as opposed to the church.

C. It developed a technical vocabulary and made use of Aristotle's philosophy and terms.

D. This vocabulary, along with the knowledge of Latin, allowed scholars to communicate quickly and concisely with one another.

II. Francis Turretin (1623–1687)

A. Turretin was a professor and pastor in the Reformed church in Geneva.

B. He wrote a three-volume work titled *The Institutes of Elenctic Theology*.
   i.   In it he deals with controversial theological topics of his day.
   ii. Through the nineteenth century, students at Princeton Seminary read Turretin in the original Latin.

III. Scholastic Precision

A. Scholastics almost always began by clarifying precisely what issue was being addressed.

B. They sought to identify the real point of disagreement between opposing views.

C. This precision was needed since they had to contend with Roman Catholics and Lutherans.

D. This precision was also needed to address intra-Reformed disagreements.

IV. Moise Amyraut

A. Amyraut was a French professor and pastor.

B. He challenged the notion that Christ died for the elect alone, teaching that Christ died for everyone.

C. His views sparked a movement that came to be called Amyraldianism, sometimes also called "four-point Calvinism."

D. Amyraut made his case very pointedly, and had to have a precise kind of answer to what he was doing.

V. The French Reformed Church in the Seventeenth Century

A. The French reformed were a minority and had to decide whether to be prudent or firm.
   i.   Being prudent meant making Calvinism as attractive and least offensive as possible.
   ii. Being firm meant upholding Reformed distinctives without compromise.

B. Neither strategy ultimately worked, and from 1600–1670 it shrank to half its size.

C. In the 1680s, Louis XIV revoked the Edict of Nantes, which allowed Calvinists to be tolerated, and many French Huguenots moved abroad.

VI. The Value of Scholastic Theology

A. There has long been a misconception that scholastic theology is dead and unhelpful, but in the past few decades it has become more appreciated.

B. There is now a flourishing again of an appreciation for scholastic writing, much of which is being translated into English.

C. Scholastic theologians were also very concerned about piety.

STUDY QUESTIONS

1. Scholastic theology refers to theology that developed in _____.
   a. The church
   b. Institutions of education
   c. Monasteries
   d. Guilds

2. In the seventeenth century, scholars could easily communicate with one another in Latin.
   a. True
   b. False

3. Seventeenth century scholastic theology depended heavily upon the philosophy of _____.
   a. Aristotle
   b. Plato
   c. Socrates
   d. Plotinus

4. The movement known as Amyraldianism is often called "four-point Calvinism."
   a. True
   b. False

5. Francis Turretin wrote what may be the pinnacle of Reformed scholastic theology, a three volume work titled, _____.
   a. Institutes of the Christian Religion
   b. Institutes of Elenctic Theology
   c. Reformed Dogmatics
   d. The Christian's Reasonable Service

DISCUSSION QUESTIONS

1. Scholastic theologians almost always began their debates by ascertaining the state of the question. How can their methodology help in everyday conversations?

2. Amyraut argued for what some might have considered a minor theological issue. However, his teaching had widespread repercussions. How can Christians approach seemingly trivial issues with gentleness and love?

3. Dr. Godfrey comments that Turretin knew the difference between scholastic theology and preaching, and that he didn't take his theology book into the pulpit to read. In what ways should your discussion of the faith remain the same, and yet differ, when talking with Christians and non-Christians of various levels of education? How important is humility in any such situation?

4. What are some ways that scholastic theology might benefit the church today? Are there areas in your own understanding of theology where you could benefit from their precision?

3

Puritan Piety

MESSAGE INTRODUCTION

Inward apathy toward the Lord masked by outward obedience is a real and constant threat in any church. Keenly aware of this danger, the Puritans zealously proclaimed the importance of heart-felt affection for the Lord. They sought to nourish genuine faith and piety especially through passionate preaching, Bible studies, and conscientious Sabbath observance. Though frequently portrayed as joyless legalists, we will see in this lesson that in reality, Puritans were more frequently characterized by their pursuit of joyful, sincere devotion to the Lord.

SCRIPTURE READINGS

Exodus 20:8–11; Psalm 51:15–17

TEACHING OBJECTIVES

1. To highlight the Puritans' great concern for faith, devotion, and piety
2. To show the emphasis Puritans placed on preaching to the heart
3. To explain why most of the English-speaking world of the seventeenth century kept the Christian Sabbath

QUOTATION

As it is the law of nature, that, in general, a due proportion of time be set apart for the worship of God; so, in his Word, by a positive, moral, and perpetual commandment binding all men in all ages, he hath particularly appointed one day in seven, for a Sabbath, to be kept holy unto him: which, from the beginning of the world to the resurrection of Christ, was the last day of the week; and, from the resurrection of Christ, was changed into the first day of the week, which, in Scripture, is called the Lord's day, and is to be continued to the end of the world, as the Christian Sabbath.

—*Westminster Confession of Faith 21.7*

LECTURE OUTLINE

I.   The Emergence of the Puritans

    A. The sixteenth century saw great change in the organization and theology of the church.

    B. In the seventeenth century there was a concern to promote faith, piety, and devotion in the hearts of the people.

        i. This was desired to combat formalism, where people and churches have the externals right, but are inwardly placid.

        ii. Puritanism was one movement that was greatly concerned about piety.

    C. Puritanism is an English phenomenon, but it had great impact beyond England.

        i. It began as a movement in the Church of England.

        ii. Many felt that reform within the Church of England hadn't gone far enough.

    D. Puritans wanted to promote genuine piety in a situation where almost everyone was part of the Church of England and was required to go to church.

        i. To this end, they sought to preach in order to affect the hearts of the hearers.

        ii. They established "lectureships," which were similar to Bible studies, so that people would understand Scripture better.

II. Puritans and the Sabbath

    A. Another major concern of the Puritans was the observance of the Christian Sabbath.

    B. They were persuaded that Scripture taught the necessity of the Sabbath, and that it was necessary for the spiritual well-being of the church.

    C. They sought to persuade everyone to rest from their labors and devote themselves to the things of God.

    D. By the middle of the seventeenth century, the English-speaking world was mostly Sabbatarian.

    E. From the seventeenth century into the twentieth, one of the real marks of conservative Protestantism was a commitment to the Sabbath.

    F. King James I wanted his subjects to play sports on Sunday, so as to be fit for military service, but the Puritans fought against this and won.

III. William Perkins

    A. Perkins is one of the foundational Puritan theologians.

    B. He lived and ministered under Queen Elizabeth.

    C. He wrote one of the most influential books on preaching titled *The Art of Prophesying*.

        i. He emphasized not only expositing the Word, but also *applying* it.

        ii. He explained how it was necessary to take into consideration the different hearers in the audience, whether strong Christians, weak Christians, or the unconverted.

IV. Puritan Hopes for Reform
   A. The Puritans had hoped that Queen Elizabeth would lead reform, but this didn't happen.
   B. Reign passed to James, who had been raised by Presbyterian tutors in Scotland.
      i. He didn't like Presbyterians because they didn't have sufficient respect for the king.
      ii. Rather than make the Church of England more like the Church of Scotland, James and his son Charles I made the Church of Scotland more like the Church of England.

STUDY QUESTIONS

   1. A major concern of the seventeenth century was _____, where churchgoers observed external religious rites scrupulously, but did not have true devotion to God in their lives and hearts.
      a. Nominalism
      b. Formalism
      c. Atheism
      d. Existentialism

   2. Puritanism began as a movement in the Church of England.
      a. True
      b. False

   3. The Puritans established _____, which were similar to today's Bible studies, with the exception that only one person usually spoke.
      a. Home groups
      b. Discipleship groups
      c. Conferences
      d. Lectureships

   4. In seventeenth-century England, almost everyone belonged to the Church of England.
      a. True
      b. False

   5. The best, single, brief summary of Puritan theology is _____.
      a. The Westminster Confession of Faith
      b. The Belgic Confession
      c. The Marrow of Divinity
      d. The Canons of Dort

DISCUSSION QUESTIONS

1. Does your church emphasize the idea of Sunday as a Christian Sabbath? How does observing the Sabbath tie in with the Puritan emphasis on piety?

2. From a biblical perspective, what is wrong with formalism?

3. In the seventeenth century, the law in England required church attendance. Do you think that this contributed to the problem of formalism? In our day, should parents require their older children to attend church? Why or why not?

4

Puritan Politics

MESSAGE INTRODUCTION

During the mid-seventeenth century, England was embroiled in a civil war between the king's forces and those of parliament. The aftermath of this conflict saw political change and much theological reflection. It was during this time period that the Westminster Assembly met to reform doctrine, church government, and worship. In this lecture, you will study this tumultuous time period, focusing on the connection between the Puritans and politics. You will also come to a better understanding of the climate within which the Westminster Assembly took place.

SCRIPTURE READINGS

1 Timothy 2:1–4

TEACHING OBJECTIVES

1. To explain the turbulent political history of the mid-seventeenth century
2. To show how Calvinism challenged monarchical rule
3. To explain the reason for and goals of the Westminster Assembly, as well as its outcomes

QUOTATION

God, the supreme Lord and King of all the world, hath ordained civil magistrates, to be, under him, over the people, for his own glory, and the public good: and, to this end, hath armed them with the power of the sword, for the defense and encouragement of them that are good, and for the punishment of evildoers.

It is the duty of people to pray for magistrates, to honor their persons, to pay them tribute or other dues, to obey their lawful commands, and to be subject to their authority, for conscience' sake. Infidelity, or difference in religion, doth not make void the magistrates' just and legal authority, nor free the people from their due obedience to them:

*from which ecclesiastical persons are not exempted, much less hath the pope any power
and jurisdiction over them in their dominions, or over any of their people; and, least of
all, to deprive them of their dominions, or lives, if he shall judge them to be heretics, or
upon any other pretense whatsoever.*

—*Westminster Confession of Faith 23.1, 4*

LECTURE OUTLINE

I. The Puritans as a Major Social and Political Power

    A. There were some in England who began to side with the Puritans mainly for political reasons.

    B. Throughout Europe, Calvinism became the ideology of many who advocated for decentralized government.

        i. Puritanism became a political issue over and against the king.

        ii. Puritans increasingly identified themselves with parliament and its claims to authority.

II. King Charles I and Parliament

    A. When Charles I became king, he wanted to rule without parliament.

    B. Charles sought to keep the Puritan faction under control.

    C. He made William Laud, who hated the Puritans, the bishop of London.

    D. The Scots rallied around a document called "The National Covenant."

        i. They covenanted with Christ to maintain Reformed doctrine, church government, and worship.

        ii. As many as 50 percent of all the people in Scotland signed the covenant.

    E. In 1640, the king finally called Parliament with the hope of raising taxes.

    F. The Parliament was dominated by Puritans, so he sent them home (this became known as "The Short Parliament").

    G. Later that year, Charles called another Parliament, which was again filled with Puritans.

    H. He tried to send them home, but they refused (called "The Long Parliament" because it remained in session 20 years).

III. Civil War

    A. In 1642, civil war broke out in England between the king and parliament.

[handwritten annotation: king's rule ↙ ↙ Christs' rule above "king" and "parliament"]

    B. Parliament found allies in Scotland and Ireland, entering into "The Solemn League and Covenant" in 1643.

    C. Oliver Cromwell became the leader of the parliamentary forces.

        i. He developed a disciplined army that became known as "The New Model Army."

        ii. Cromwell's forces were successful in fighting the king's army.

    D. The king was forced to surrender.

    E. In 1646 Charles I was arrested, and in 1649 he was executed as a tyrant.

[handwritten annotation: — Don't mess with the Puritans!]

IV. The Ascendance of Cromwell

    A. Parliament was made up mostly of Presbyterians who wanted to make the Anglican Church a Presbyterian church.

    B. Cromwell was a Congregationalist and thought independent churches were needed.

    C. Cromwell eventually became "Lord Protector of the Commonwealth," and promoted congregationalism, which prevented England from ever having a national Presbyterian church.

V. After Cromwell

    A. When Cromwell died, the Commonwealth disintegrated, and Charles II was restored to the throne.

    B. Charles II was supported by the Scots because he had promised to maintain their church.

    C. The moment he came to the throne, he repudiated his promise and began to persecute the Scots.

    D. Charles II threw the Puritans out of the Church of England.

VI. Benefits from the War

    A. Monarchs in England never regained their ability to rule without parliament.

    B. Parliament established an assembly of theologians and ministers to decide how to reform the church, which became known as "The Westminster Assembly."

        i. It was not a church assembly.

        ii. It was a parliamentary committee.

    C. The Westminster Assembly wanted to reform the church in three ways.

        i. They wanted a clear statement of Reformed theology.

            1. They made a confession of faith.

            2. They wrote a larger catechism for adults and a shorter catechism for children.

        ii. They wanted a clear direction on Reformed worship.

        iii. They wanted a clear Reformed government for the life of the church.

STUDY QUESTIONS

1. _____ became the ideology of many who advocated for decentralized government in the seventeenth century.

    a. Absolutism

    b. Socialism

    c. Calvinism

    d. Arminianism

2. King Charles I encouraged a Presbyterian form of church government in England.

    a. True

    b. False

3. The Scots rallied around a document called _____, in which they promised to maintain Reformed doctrine, church government, and worship.
    a. The National Covenant
    b. The Westminster Confession
    c. The National Promise
    d. The Declaration of 1638

4. When Oliver Cromwell died, Charles II was restored to the throne.
    a. True
    b. False

5. The Westminster Assembly was a _____.
    a. Church assembly
    b. Parliamentary committee
    c. Ecumenical council
    d. Presbyterian assembly

DISCUSSION QUESTIONS

1. Explain why the Westminster Assembly created a longer and a shorter catechism. Does this have any relevance for how teaching should be done to different groups at home or in the church?

2. How did Puritanism become viewed as a way of opposing the king?

3. Explain the change in leadership from Charles I to Charles II.

4. As read by Dr. Godfrey, question 77 of the Westminster Larger Catechism asks, "Wherein do justification and sanctification differ?" Respond to this question.

5

Puritan Worship and Eschatology

MESSAGE INTRODUCTION

Many Reformed churches today trace their roots back to the Puritans, and have even adopted as their standards the Westminster Confession and Catechisms. However, there are two areas where most of those churches differ from their Puritan predecessors: worship and eschatology. In this lecture, Dr. Godfrey explains why the Puritans worshipped the way did, and how they understood the book of Revelation.

SCRIPTURE READINGS

1 John 2:18; Revelation 20:1–6

TEACHING OBJECTIVES

1. To explain the Puritan approach to worship, especially regarding instruments and the use of Psalms
2. To highlight the ways the Puritans read the book of Revelation
3. To show the diversity of opinions among puritans on the nature of the millennium

QUOTATIONS

The light of nature showeth that there is a God, who hath lordship and sovereignty over all, is good, and doth good unto all, and is therefore to be feared, loved, praised, called upon, trusted in, and served, with all the heart, and with all the soul, and with all the might. But the acceptable way of worshiping the true God is instituted by himself, and so limited by his own revealed will, that he may not be worshiped according to the imaginations and devices of men, or the suggestions of Satan, under any visible representation, or any other way not prescribed in the Holy Scripture.

—*Westminster Confession of Faith 21.1*

As Christ would have us to be certainly persuaded that there shall be a day of judgment, both to deter all men from sin; and for the greater consolation of the godly in their adversity: so will he have that day unknown to men, that they may shake off all carnal security, and be always watchful, because they know not at what hour the Lord will come; and may be ever prepared to say, Come Lord Jesus, come quickly, Amen.

—Westminster Confession of Faith 33.3

LECTURE OUTLINE

I.   Origin of the Westminster Assembly

    A.   The Westminster Assembly was instructed by parliament to find a way to reform and improve the Church of England.

    B.   They were to reform doctrine, which they did with the Westminster Confession and catechisms.

    C.   They were to reform church government.

        i.   They spent considerable time discussing how church government should run.

        ii. Ultimately, they were unable to reconcile Congregationalism and Presbyterianism.

    D.   They were to reform worship.

        i.   The Puritans had little trouble reforming worship, because they simply followed the directions of John Calvin.

        ii. Worship had to be Bible-driven and Bible-instructed.

            1.   For Calvin and the Puritans, this meant no musical instruments.

            2.   It was agreed on that only Psalms should be sung in worship.

II. Eschatology at the Westminster Assembly

    A.   There was a great diversity of opinions among the Puritans concerning the end times and the coming of Christ.

    B.   There were some things on which all Puritans agreed.

        i.   All Puritans agreed that the antichrist is the pope.

        ii. They agreed on how the book of Revelation is to be read.

            1.   It is to be read as a prophecy of the whole history of the church.

            2.   The goal is to figure out where in the book we are.

            3.   They thought you could calculate roughly when Jesus would return.

            4.   After the civil war, many Congregationalists thought the end was almost near.

    C.   By the seventeenth century, many English Puritans began to see Christ not just as the builder of the church, but also the glorifier.

        i.   They believed Christ would give the church earthly glory to dominate the world spiritually.

        ii. They saw the future as a coming golden age when Christ would be glorified on earth.

       iii. This view, closely tied to postmillenialism, became the dominante view within the Reformed tradition in the seventeenth, eighteenth, and nineteenth centuries.

       iv. Despite how widespread this view was, not everybody believed it, and so the Westminster Confession doesn't require it.

    D. The view of Christ as rescuer of the church (premillenialism) didn't become dominant in America until the early twentieth century.

       i.   This view sees the church as under attack and waiting to be rescued out of the evil world.

       ii. There were some already in the seventeenth century who held this view, but they were a minority.

III. The Puritans as great writers of spiritual devotion.

    A. The most famous spiritual writing is John Bunyan's book, *Pilgrims Progress*.

    B. For several centuries it was probably the most widely read book after the Bible.

STUDY QUESTIONS

1. There was consensus among Puritans on the matter of _____ because there was common agreement with the teaching of John Calvin.

    a. Worship

    b. Church government

    c. Eschatology

    d. The use of images

2. The Puritans encouraged the use of instruments in church worship.

    a. True

    b. False

3. Dr. Godfrey thinks that many Christians are too "pious" to use the words of Psalm _____ when praying or singing to God.

    a. 119

    b. 77

    c. 19

    d. 84

4. In the sixteenth, seventeenth, and eighteenth centuries, nearly all Protestants believed that the pope was the antichrist.

    a. True

    b. False

5. _____ dominated the Reformed churches of the seventeenth through nine-teenth centuries.
   a. Premillenialism
   b. Postmillenialism
   c. Amillenialism
   d. Panmillenialism

DISCUSSION QUESTIONS

1. Explain the argument for only using Psalms in worship. Do you find this persuasive? Why or why not?

2. Read Psalm 88 and reflect on the boldness with which the psalmist speaks to God. Are you this open in your prayers to the Lord? How can we best approach God with boldness and yet reverence?

3. Dr. Godfrey mentions that the Puritan way to read Revelation has largely been abandoned. How can reflecting on this cultivate humility in our interpretations of the more difficult passages of Scripture?

4. Do you find the argument against using instruments compelling? How is one's conviction that instruments shouldn't be used in worship tied to one's conviction that only Psalms should be sung?

6

Puritan Views of Assurance and Conversion

MESSAGE INTRODUCTION

Assurance of one's salvation is an important part of Protestant faith, and one of the many marks that sharply distinguishes it from Roman Catholicism. In the seventeenth century, however, many within Puritan circles struggled with this issue. In this lecture, Dr. Godfrey will explain this struggle. He will also spend considerable time discussing the Puritan understanding of conversion, and will show that the very idea of conversion has changed dramatically over the past few centuries.

SCRIPTURE READINGS

Romans 8:28–30; Galatians 2:15–16

TEACHING OBJECTIVES

1. To explore the importance to which some Puritans ascribed the doctrine of assurance
2. To explain the change in meaning of the word *conversion*, and how it has impacted Christians' understanding of justification
3. To look at the start of Protestant missions

QUOTATION

Although hypocrites and other unregenerate men may vainly deceive themselves with false hopes and carnal presumptions of being in the favor of God, and estate of salvation (which hope of theirs shall perish): yet such as truly believe in the Lord Jesus, and love him in sincerity, endeavoring to walk in all good conscience before him, may, in this life, be certainly assured that they are in the state of grace, and may rejoice in the hope of the glory of God, which hope shall never make them ashamed.

This infallible assurance doth not so belong to the essence of faith, but that a true believer may wait long, and conflict with many difficulties before he be partaker of it: yet, being enabled by the Spirit to know the things which are freely given him of God, he may, without extraordinary revelation, in the right use of ordinary means, attain thereunto. And therefore it is the duty of everyone to give all diligence to make his calling and election sure, that thereby his heart may be enlarged in peace and joy in the Holy Ghost, in love and thankfulness to God, and in strength and cheerfulness in the duties of obedience, the proper fruits of this assurance; so far is it from inclining men to looseness.

—Westminster Confession of Faith 18.1, 3

LECTURE OUTLINE

I. The Puritans and Assurance of Salvation
    A. The Roman Catholic theologian Robert Bellarmine said that the worst Protestant heresy was the doctrine of the perseverance of the saints.
    B. For many Protestants, assurance is part of the essential joy of being a Christian.
    C. The great theme of assurance was preached by the early Reformers.
    D. By the seventeenth century, in Puritan circles, assurance became something of a problem for some.
        i.   Some expressed that they wanted to believe, but that they were not sure if they did.
        ii. Puritan pastors responded by trying to separate faith from assurance.
        iii. These pastors taught that it was possible to have peace with God (faith) without knowing it (assurance).
        iv. Separating faith and assurance actually led to a growing problem of assurance.
            1. The Westminster Standards were written so that those who think assurance is of the essence of the faith can subscribe, and those who don't can as well.
            2. The Heidelberg Catechism reflects the belief that assurance is essential to the faith.

II. The Meaning of Conversion
    A. In the sixteenth century, conversion meant sanctification.
    B. A treatise on conversion in the early part of the seventeenth century was a treatise on sanctification.
    C. Conversion is rooted in the Latin word for turning, and was an idea about the whole of the Christian life, which is turning to God.

III. Conversion in the Eighteenth Century.
    A. Moving into the eighteenth century, conversion began to take on a more technical meaning of the beginning of the Christian life.

B. This is significant because it may be that in a lot of American religion in the nineteenth century, less attention was given to the question, "Do you have faith and are you justified?" and more time was given to the question, "Are you converted?"

C. There seems to have been a shift from justification as the foundational concern of the Christian life to conversion, which is really an issue of sanctification.

   i. This can lead to moralizing.

   ii. It is why many today are confused about justification.

IV. The Puritans and the Monarchy

   A. The restoration of the monarchy took place in 1660.

   B. Many believed that Puritanism should not dominate the country.

   C. In the Church of England, they wanted a purer Anglican theology to dominate.

V. The Church of England Confronts Immorality

   A. Confronted by immorality, the Church of England preached law and holiness.

   B. A movement arose called "moralism," or "neonomianism."

   i. They thought lawlessness was best addressed by preaching the law.

   ii. Jeremy Taylor said that one is not a child of God if they knowingly and deliberately do something God hates.

   iii. This theology turned into people trusting themselves and relying on what they could accomplish.

VI. The Beginning of Protestant Missions

   A. Protestant missions essentially began in the seventeenth century.

   B. The Catholics had been going on missionary endeavors with the Spanish and Portuguese.

   C. Protestant missionary opportunities first opened up with the Dutch and the British as they expanded to different countries for trade.

STUDY QUESTIONS

1. The Roman Catholic theologian Robert Bellarmine said that the doctrine of _____ was the worst heresy of the Protestants.

   a. Predestination

   b. The perseverance of the saints

   c. Election

   d. Infant baptism

2. The Westminster Standards teach that assurance is of the essence of faith.

   a. True

   b. False

3. The English word *conversion* is rooted in the Latin word for _____.
   a. Conversation
   b. Turning
   c. Letting go
   d. Sorrow

4. After the English civil war, Anglicans combatted the immorality they saw by preaching grace and forgiveness.
   a. True
   b. False

5. Protestant missionary opportunities began to open up in the seventeenth century with the growth of Dutch and _____ trade.
   a. American
   b. British
   c. Canadian
   d. French

DISCUSSION QUESTIONS

1. How important is the doctrine of assurance for your faith? What passage(s) of Scripture can be a comfort when you or a fellow believer are struggling in this regard?

2. Dr. Godfrey argues that changes in a word's meaning can subtly affect our thinking. How has the change in meaning of the word *conversion* affected the emphasis on and importance of justification?

3. Summarize and critique the moralistic or neonomian movement of the latter part of the seventeenth century.

4. Explain the origin of Protestant missions within the Reformed church.

7

The Puritans in New England

MESSAGE INTRODUCTION

When the Puritans came to the New World, they had no intention of establishing a new religion. What they did want to do, however, was bring their old world religious ideal into reality. Despite the inherent difficulties in their new environment, the Puritans found some measure of early success. But as time passed, internal challenges added to the external. In this lecture, Dr. Godfrey will summarize the religious foundations of the American colonies, looking especially at the Puritans' desire to maintain a pure church.

SCRIPTURE READINGS

Matthew 5:14; Micah 6:6–8

TEACHING OBJECTIVES

1. To highlight the Puritans' hopes in coming to the New World
2. To highlight early Puritan efforts among the American Indians
3. To explain the difficulties that arose over church membership

QUOTATION

Now the only way to avoid this shipwreck, and to provide for our posterity, is to follow the counsel of Micah, to do justly, to love mercy, to walk humbly with our God. For this end, we must be knit together, in this work, as one man. We must entertain each other in brotherly affection. We must be willing to abridge ourselves of our superfluities, for the supply of others' necessities. We must uphold a familiar commerce together in all meekness, gentleness, patience and liberality. We must delight in each other; make others' conditions our own; rejoice together, mourn together, labor and suffer together, always having before our eyes our commission and community in the work, as members of the same body. So shall we keep the unity of the spirit in the bond of peace. The Lord will be our God, and

*delight to dwell among us, as His own people, and will command a blessing upon us in all
our ways, so that we shall see much more of His wisdom, power, goodness and truth, than
formerly we have been acquainted with. We shall find that the God of Israel is among us,
when ten of us shall be able to resist a thousand of our enemies; when He shall make us a
praise and glory that men shall say of succeeding plantations, "may the Lord make it like
that of New England." For we must consider that we shall be as a city upon a hill.*

—John Winthrop

LECTURE OUTLINE

I. Foundations of Religion in the American Colonies

   A. The Puritans didn't come to the New World to do anything new.

   B. They came to bring an improved version of the old world.

   C. In New England the desire to realize the Puritan ideal of the old world was especially intense.

II. Hope for Religious Improvement

   A. Puritans thought that more rapid improvement could take place in the New World.

   B. They believed they could have a real role in redemptive history, and that they could even hasten the coming of Christ.

   C. They thought Christ would glorify His church.

   D. Some who came were separatists.

      i. They gave up on the Church of England.

      ii. They self-consciously separated themselves from the Church of England.

   E. Most were non-separating Congregationalists.

      i. They didn't say the Church of England was a false church, and they didn't formally separate.

      ii. But they did not conform to the practices of the Church of England.

         1. They didn't have a bishop.

         2. They didn't use the Book of Common Prayer.

         3. They didn't wear vestments.

   F. The Puritans wanted to have a pure, state church.

      i. They were not interested in religious toleration.

      ii. They were committed to the congregational church.

      iii. To vote in political elections, one had to be a member of the established Congregational church.

III. The Reality of Religious Improvement

   A. For the first 10 or 20 years this worked well because most were motivated to come to the New World because of religious devotion.

      i. They founded the first college in 1638, which was called Harvard.

      ii. It was a Calvinist college founded to train Calvinist minsters.

B. They began to get involved with missions to American Indians.
   i. There was great success in certain tribes early on.
   ii. Evangelization was on the rise until the colony shifted from being fundamentally religious to commercial.

IV. Challenges to Religious Improvement
   A. Problems began to develop, as the younger generation was not as enthusiastic about religion as the first generation.
   B. This lead to the question of how to ensure the next generation is as faithful as the first.
   C. It intensified the question about what should be required of someone to be a church member.
   D. Many Puritans began looking for a testimony of grace in the believer's life, as they went from rebellion to faith.
   E. There were different opinions about how strict church membership requirements should be.
      i. Richard Mather said, "Better we should exclude ten real Christians from the church than admit one non-Christian."
      ii. John Cotton said, "Better to let ten non-Christians into the church than to keep one true Christian out."
   F. In 1684 the King revoked the charter under which the colony operated.
      i. The old charter had allowed them to operate essentially as they saw fit.
      ii. The new charter imposed a governor.
      iii. It made voting a matter of property ownership rather than church membership.
   G. In 1692 the Salem Witchcraft Trials took place.
      i. The Puritan ministers were mostly trying to keep the hysteria under control.
      ii. Many common people felt that the devil himself was attacking their society and possessing five women who were ultimately executed.

STUDY QUESTIONS

1. The Puritans who came to Plymouth were mostly _____.
   a. Separating Puritans
   b. Non-separating Puritans
   c. Neonomians
   d. Anglicans

2. The Puritans who founded the Massachusetts Bay Colony fully separated from the Church of England.
   a. True
   b. False

3. The main motivation for people coming to New England early on was _____.
    a. Farming
    b. Trade
    c. Religious devotion
    d. Availability of land

4. Harvard College was founded primarily for the purpose of training Calvinist minsters.
    a. True
    b. False

5. When the king created a new charter, voting became based on _____.
    a. Church membership
    b. Ownership of property
    c. Place of birth
    d. A minimum holding of money

DISCUSSION QUESTIONS

1. Dr. Godfrey notes that some of the Puritans who came to America separated from the Church of England, while others did not. When do you think a group has grounds to separate from the wider community of faith? What biblical basis do you have for this?

2. Evangelization among American Indians grew until the colonies went in a more commercial direction. How can this shift serve as a warning for churches and even individuals today?

3. A major issue that Puritans had to deal with was the decline in religious enthusiasm among subsequent generations. How can churches and parents best encourage devotion in their children?

4. Explain how the Salem Witchcraft Trials may have been affected by societal tensions of the time. Do you find this explanation more satisfying than traditional narratives of the trials?

8

The Enlightenment

MESSAGE INTRODUCTION

The Enlightenment had a profound effect on Western thought. During this period, some sought to reconcile the Christian faith with modern thought, while others tried to cut themselves completely from their Christian moorings. But even those who set out to uproot the Christian influence upon society ended up adopting suspiciously similar ideas. In this lecture, Dr. Godfrey will show us how the church navigated through the Enlightenment, pointing out the different responses to this new challenge.

SCRIPTURE READINGS

Romans 3:9–20; John 15:5

TEACHING OBJECTIVES

1. To explain how the Enlightenment affected Christianity in the West
2. To show the shift in thinking from religion to humanism
3. To examine the fundamental beliefs shared by Enlightenment philosophers

QUOTATION

As men, we have God for our King, and are under the law of reason: as Christians, we have Jesus the Messiah for our King, and are under the law revealed by him in the gospel. And though every Christian, both as a deist and a Christian, be obliged to study both the law of nature and the revealed law, that in them he may know the will of God, and of Jesus Christ, whom he hath sent; yet, in neither of these laws, is there to be found a select set of fundamentals, distinct from the rest, which are to make him a deist, or a Christian. But he that believes one eternal, invisible God, his Lord and King, ceases thereby to be an atheist ; and he that believes Jesus to be the Messiah, his king, ordained by God, thereby becomes a Christian, is delivered from the power of darkness, and is translated into the kingdom of the Son of God ; is actually within the covenant of grace, and has that faith, which shall be imputed to him for righteousness; and, if he continues in his allegiance to this his King, shall receive the reward: eternal life.

—John Locke

LECTURE OUTLINE

I. Emerging Perspectives on the Christian Faith

    A. In Europe, different views were emerging as to what it meant to be a Christian.

    B. They were seemingly drifting away from Christianity.

    C. Many who sought to redefine Christianity thought they were serving the interest of Christianity.

II. European Unity Sought outside the Church

    A. In the middle ages, the Church gave Europeans a sense of unity.

    B. After the Church divided during the Reformation, some began to look to the "principles of Christianity" as the way to unity.

III. From Religion to Humanism

    A. In 1695 the political philosopher John Locke wrote a book called *The Reasonableness of Christianity*.

        i. He claimed to defend Christianity.

        ii. He talked about how reason can lead us to many of the conclusions that Christianity comes to, and that these reasonable parts can unite us all on a political as well as cultural level.

    B. In 1696 the deist John Toland came out with a work which argued that since we can come to the important parts of Christianity ourselves, we don't really need the Bible.

    C. There is a shift from religion in the direction of a kind of humanism.

    D. Human beings, without revelation from God, can arrive at the fundamental ethics needed to bind us all together.

    E. Increasingly among leaders of the Enlightenment, particularly in France, there was a growing, radical notion that Christianity (in the form of Roman Catholicism) has a negative impact on the modern world.

IV. The Secularization of Christian Ideas

    A. The Enlightenment was foundational to the secularization of the West.

    B. Carl Becker argued in the 1930's that what happened in the Enlightenment was that fundamental Christian ideas were simply secularized.

        i. In many ways, one could say the Enlightenment was just a Christian heresy.

        ii. It pirated a lot of what Christianity teaches and believes without giving credit to God.

iii. Becker helps show how an age is dominated by certain ideas, ideals, and slogans.
1. For the Enlightenment
    a. Man is not natively depraved.
    b. The end/goal of life is life itself, the good life on earth.
    c. Man is capable, guided solely by the light of reason and experience, of perfecting the good life on earth.
    d. The first and essential condition of the good life on earth is the freeing of men's minds from the bonds of ignorance and superstition, and their bodies from arbitrary oppression of the constituted social authorities.
2. What keeps us back is not sinfulness but superstition.
iv. The foundation laid in the Enlightenment had a huge impact on the development of Western thinking for the next three centuries.
v. There was a desire to find unity and focus on making current life better, rather than focusing on the world to come—this appealed to many people.

V. Problems with Church Membership
A. In 1662 the churches came up with the "halfway covenant."
B. There were many married people who had children but hadn't joined the church.
    i. They wanted to have their kids baptized.
    ii. You couldn't have your children baptized if you weren't church members.
    iii. If members had been baptized, they were permitted to present their children for baptism.
C. Solomon Stoddard went further and argued that members who hadn't professed their faith publically should be permitted to come to the Lord's Supper.
D. He thought it was a converting ordinance and those who took it might get converted.

STUDY QUESTIONS

1. The political philosopher _____ wrote a book arguing that human reason can lead to many of the same conclusions as the Christian faith.
    a. John Locke
    b. Jean-Jacques Rousseau
    c. Thomas Hobbes
    d. David Hume

2. In France, the Enlightenment animosity towards Christianity was directed primarily at the Roman Catholic Church.
    a. True
    b. False

3. The historian Carl Becker argued that in the Enlightenment, Christian ideas were simply being _____.
    a. Ignored
    b. Accepted
    c. Secularized
    d. Demonized

4. The Enlightenment saw superstition, rather than sinfulness, as a major impediment to living the good life on earth.
    a. True
    b. False

5. _____ allowed baptized, non-members of New England churches to have their own children baptized.
    a. The Abrahamic covenant
    b. The "halfway covenant"
    c. The agreement of 1662
    d. The Infant Initiative

BIBLE STUDY AND DISCUSSION QUESTIONS

1. John Locke tried to show how reason could lead to many of the same conclusions as Christianity. Do you think his attempt to do so was helpful? Why or why not?

2. According to Carl Becker's thesis about the Enlightenment, what are some ways that Enlightenment era philosophers adopted and secularized Christian ideas?

3. Compare and contrast the central commitments of Enlightenment religion with the Christian faith.

4. Explain what led to the "halfway covenant." How has societal pressure affected you or your church's beliefs?

9

Wesley and Whitefield

MESSAGE INTRODUCTION

The religious climate in England in the late seventeenth and early eighteenth centuries was cold and dry. Onto this barren landscape came George Whitefield and John Wesley, whose powerful preaching and novel methods played an important role in kindling hearts and stirring religious affection. In this lecture, Dr. Godfrey will introduce both of these men, the spiritual context within which they worked, and the results of their ministries.

SCRIPTURE READINGS

Romans 1:16–17; 1 Corinthians 1:18–19

TEACHING OBJECTIVES

1. To introduce the background and early work of George Whitefield and Charles Wesley
2. To examine the impact that both men's ministries had
3. To show how revolutionary their approach to ministry was

QUOTATIONS

It is no marvel that the devil does not love field preaching! Neither do I; I love a commodious room, a soft cushion, a handsome pulpit. But where is my zeal if I do not trample all these underfoot in order to save one more soul?

—John Wesley

True conversion means turning not only from sin but also from depending on self-made righteousness. Those who trust in their own righteousness for conversion hide behind their own good works. This is the reason that self-righteous people are so angry with gospel preachers, because the gospel does not spare those who will not submit to the righteousness of Jesus Christ!

—George Whitefield

LECTURE OUTLINE

I.   The Decline of Religion and Morality in England

   A.   By the early eighteenth century, religious and moral life in England was reaching a fairly low point.

   B.   Sexual immorality and drunkenness were becoming a great problem.

   C.   The Church of England seemed paralyzed to help in any way.

   D.   Many people felt that there needed to be a religious renewal.

II. John Wesley and Religious Renewal

   A.   Wesley's father was a minister in the Church of England.

   B.   Wesley attended Oxford University.

   C.   With his younger brother, Charles, he formed a "holy club."

      i.   They read the Bible together in Greek and Hebrew.

      ii.   They sought diligently to serve the Lord and to be faithful.

   D.   In 1735 he decided to be a missionary in Georgia among the American Indians.

      i.   Going across the Atlantic, his ship encountered a severe storm.

      ii.   He was challenged by the faith of a group of Moravian Christians.

      iii. After three years he returned to England, and a church sermon that focused on justification is thought to be the moment of conversion in his life.

III. George Whitefield's Influence on Wesley

   A.   They attended Oxford together, though Whitefield was 11 years younger.

   B.   Whitefield pioneered in open air preaching, something that was regarded as beneath the dignity of a clergyman of the Church of England.

   C.   People in England were moving to new regions of England where there were no churches yet built.

      i.   There was no one to minister to these growing populations.

      ii.   Whitefield began to preach to them.

      iii. Whitefield decided to go to Georgia and asked John Wesley to take over the open air preaching, and John agreed.

      iv.   Wesley was hesitant because it was quite radical—stepping out of a church building and pulpit to preach.

IV. The Preaching of Whitefield and Wesley

   A.   Whitefield was an extraordinarily powerful preacher.

   B.   John Wesley was not known to be as great a preacher as Whitefield, but he had tremendous energy.

   C.   It's estimated that Wesley preached 40,000 sermons over his lifetime.

   D.   Whitefield and Wesley began to see real responsiveness to their preaching—it seemed that the Spirit of God was at work.

   E.   Their message was in a sense revolutionary.

    i.   In Puritan circles of the late seventeenth and early eighteenth-centuries, there was an emphasis on waiting until the Spirit had applied the law of God to one's heart—showing them their sin. Only then could one appropriately come to God.

    ii. Whitefield and Wesley, like Luther and Calvin, preached the immediacy of coming to Christ.

STUDY QUESTIONS

1. _____ Wesley, John's brother, eventually became a minister and a great hymn writer.
   a. Simon
   b. Charles
   c. George
   d. Joseph

2. By the early eighteenth century, religious and moral life in England was reaching a fairly low point.
   a. True
   b. False

3. While at Oxford, John Wesley and his brother Charles formed a group called a _____.
   a. Bible study fellowship
   b. Holy club
   c. Society of Christian scholars
   d. Moravian order

4. Both George Whitefield and Charles Wesley spent time as missionaries in Georgia.
   a. True
   b. False

5. _____ is known to this day as one of the best preachers in the history of the Christian church.
   a. John Wesley
   b. Charles Wesley
   c. George Whitefield
   d. Jonathan Edwards

DISCUSSION QUESTIONS

1. The ministries of Whitefield and Wesley saw much fruit, even when there seemed to be little hope for revitalization. How can this encourage us in our present situation?

2. Recall Wesley's discussion with the Moravian leader. What can we learn from the fact that Wesley could call Christ the Savior of the world but couldn't really call Him his personal Savior?

3. What was so radical about Whitefield and Wesley's open air preaching?

4. How did Whitefield and Wesley's preaching differ from those Puritans who emphasized the need to wait for the Spirit's leading before coming to God?

10

The Great Awakening

MESSAGE INTRODUCTION

The Great Awakening was a time of great religious interest that began in New England and spread throughout the American colonies. It was spearheaded by the great preacher George Whitefield, and aided by America's most prominent pastor and theologian, Jonathan Edwards. In this lecture, Dr. Godfrey will explain the history of this influential movement, focusing on its key figures. He will also look back to England and revisit the ministry and influence of John Wesley during this time period.

SCRIPTURE READINGS

Joel 2:12–13; Romans 10:13–15

TEACHING OBJECTIVES

1. To explain the nature and effect of the Great Awakening
2. To clarify terms associated with the Great Awakening
3. To show Jonathan Edwards and especially George Whitefield's role in the Great Awakening

QUOTATION

The God that holds you over the pit of hell, much as one holds a spider, or some loath-some insect over the fire, abhors you, and is dreadfully provoked: his wrath towards you burns like fire; he looks upon you as worthy of nothing else, but to be cast into the fire; he is of purer eyes than to bear to have you in his sight; you are ten thousand times more abominable in his eyes, than the most hateful venomous serpent is in ours. You have offended him infinitely more than ever a stubborn rebel did his prince; and yet it is nothing but his hand that holds you from falling into the fire every moment. It is to be ascribed to nothing else, that you did not go to hell the last night; that you was suffered to awake again in this world, after you closed your eyes to sleep. And there is no other reason to be given, why you have not dropped into hell since you arose in the morning, but that God's hand has held you up.

—Jonathan Edwards

LECTURE OUTLINE

I.   The Winds of Change
   A. Change began to happen in England with Whitefield and Wesley.
   B. Change also began to take place in New England, notably with Jonathan Edwards.
       i.   He was a young minister in Northampton.
       ii. In 1733 and early 1734 he saw an unusual responsiveness to the preaching.
            1. It occurred while he was preaching on justification by faith.
            2. He called it "stirrings of the Spirit" or "the beginnings of an awakening."
                a. For the Puritans, awakening had a specific meaning.
                b. It meant that there was interest, and people seemed responsive; it did not mean that there were necessarily lots of conversions.
       iii. He wrote a revival treatise that was widely published and became very influential *A Faithful Narrative of the Surprising Work of God.*

II. The Great Awakening
   A. George Whitefield was the chief catalyst.
   B. Whitefield came to preach in New England in 1740.
   C. He said that the problem in New England was that dead men were preaching to dead men.
   D. Criticism of clergy became a repeated element of the Great Awakening.
   E. Criticism of clergy meant criticism of the parish system.
   F. In the parish system, one couldn't choose which church to attend; rather, one was part of a particular parish and went to their nearest church.
   G. It seemed that God was doing something remarkable, and one observer said that it was the greatest working of the Spirit of God since Pentecost.
   H. Whitefield and Wesley would preach once or twice in a place and then move on.
       i.   They saw great responsiveness.
       ii. Some responded with crying, screaming, or fainting.
            1. This led some to criticize the Great Awakening as too emotional.
            2. Whitefield was concerned not just with awakening, but that souls were being converted.
       iii. The awakening lasted from about 1739 to 1744, taking place all over the American colonies.

III. Wesley and Whitefield Back in England
   A. Whitefield left in 1741 to return to England and help Wesley.
   B. Wesley wouldn't cooperate with Whitefield, because he had become too Calvinistic.

    C. Wesley's theology moved in a more Arminian direction.
        i. His concern for holiness sometimes seemed to compromise his commitment to justification by faith alone.
        ii. He developed a notion of Christian perfectionism, believing it was possible, by faith, for Christians to become perfect.
    D. Wesley was a great organizer and established "Methodist Societies."
        i. They were still part of the Church of England.
        ii. Their meetings looked like worship but weren't so considered.
        iii. He set up "class meetings" where ten to fifteen Methodists would meet for study, prayer, and discipleship.
        iv. It became a very powerful movement, and Methodists split from the Church of England after Wesley's death.
        v. The Methodist church became the largest church in America by the middle of the nineteenth century.
    E. Whitefield was a better preacher than Wesley, but not a better organizer.

IV. Jonathan Edwards and the Great Awakening
    A. While Whitefield is the central figure of the Great Awakening in America, Jonathan Edwards' preaching played a major role.
    B. His most famous sermon is "Sinners in the Hands of an Angry God."
    C. It was the second time he preached the sermon, not the first, that he saw a great response.
    D. The Great Awakening was driven by the preaching of ministers to congregations other than their own.

STUDY QUESTIONS

1. Jonathan Edwards saw an unusual responsiveness from his congregation while preaching on _____.
    a. Predestination
    b. The Sovereignty of God
    c. The Holiness of God
    d. Justification by faith

2. For the Puritans, the term *awakening* was synonymous with the term *conversion*.
    a. True
    b. False

3. The chief catalyst for the awakening spreading throughout New England was _____.
    a. George Whitefield
    b. Jonathan Edwards
    c. John Wesley
    d. George Tennet

4. After John Wesley's death, the Methodists continued to function within the Church of England.
    a. True
    b. False

5. The excuse that John Wesley gave for not cooperating with George Whitefield was that Whitefield had become too _____.
    a. Arminian
    b. Calvinistic
    c. Argumentative
    d. American

DISCUSSION QUESTIONS

1. Explain how the Puritans used the term "awakening." How did they understand the relationship between awakening and conversion?

2. Dr. Godfrey mentions that some of Whitefield's success went to his head. How can we best stay humble when our ministries to others find success?

3. What are some of the dangers of a parish system? Can you think of some benefits?

4. What was Whitefield's response to those who criticized the emotional responses to his preaching? Do you think such emotional displays are appropriate? Why or why not?

11

Jonathan Edwards

MESSAGE INTRODUCTION

Jonathan Edwards has been called by some the most brilliant American who ever lived. He played an integral part in the Great Awakening, and his towering intellect was matched only by his religious devotion. In this lecture, join Dr. Godfrey as he explains the life and impact of one of the most influential individuals in American history.

SCRIPTURE READINGS

Acts 2:36–41; 2 Corinthians 3:18

TEACHING OBJECTIVES

1. To survey the life and teaching of Jonathan Edwards
2. To explain Edwards' role in the Great Awakening
3. To point out some of the difficulties in studying Edwards

QUOTATION

In the soul where Christ savingly is, there He lives. He not only lives without it, so as violently to actuate it, but He lives in it, so that the soul also is alive. Grace in the soul is as much from Christ, as the light in a glass, held out in the sunbeams, is from the sun. But this represents the manner of the communication of grace to the soul only in part; because the glass remains as it was, the nature of it not being at all changed; it is as much without any lightsomeness in its nature as ever. But the soul of a saint receives light from the Sun of Righteousness, in such a manner that its nature is changed, and it becomes properly a luminous thing; not only does the sun shine in the saints, but they also become little suns, partaking of the nature of the Fountain of their light. In this respect, the manner of their derivation of light is like that of the lamps in the tabernacle, rather than that of a reflecting glass; which, though they were lit up by fire from heaven, yet thereby became themselves burning shining things.

—Jonathan Edwards

LECTURE OUTLINE

I.   The Great Awakening's Impact on Future Church Life

    A.   It led to what has been described as "the triumph of the laity in America."

    B.   If people don't like their church, they can simply go to another.

    C.   For this reason, ministers always sense they have to listen to the laity.

    D.   It created an environment where there's much more activity on the part of the laity.

II. Jonathan Edwards' Upbringing and Conversion

    A.   Many argue that he's the smartest American who ever lived.

    B.   He was born 1703 in Connecticut.

    C.   His father was a Puritan minister.

    D.   He attended Yale, which had been started because Harvard had gone liberal.

    E.   He described his conversion as a young man as being overwhelmed by a sense of the beauty of God and the glory of God in nature.

        i.   His father would not let him join the Congregational church because he didn't think this was an adequate narration of conversion.

        ii. He did finally succeed in joining the church, but it's not clear when.

III. Edwards Enters the Ministry

    A.   He went in 1725 to accompany his grandfather in the ministry.

    B.   In 1729, his grandfather died and Edwards took over for the congregation.

    C.   He saw a great response from his congregation as the Great Awakening began in the 1740s.

    D.   He recorded much of what he saw and experienced.

    E.   A strong postmillennialist, Edwards thought the church would rise through revival and then fall again until a peak was reached when Christ would return.

    F.   By 1743, he talked about how it seemed everyone in Northampton was converted.

    G.   Edwards established in the psyche of American religion that God works through revivals, and often works through great preachers.

        i.   This is a wrong notion.

        ii. God does most of his works through the settled ministry of settled ministers in settled congregations.

IV. Waning Religious Enthusiasm

    A.   By 1745 Edwards had to admit that the religious enthusiasm was diminishing in the colonies.

    B.   A lessening of devotion was difficult for him because he was something of a perfectionist.

    C.   He spent 12 to 13 hours a day studying and writing.

    D.   He didn't understand why other Christians didn't have the same sort of commitment.

    E. The issue of church membership arose again and Edwards moved away from his grandfather's acceptance of the halfway covenant.

    F. Edwards taught that there had to be a narrative of grace, and his congregation responded by firing him.

    G. He went on to be a pastor in Stockbridge, a frontier town, and he wrote many important works there.

V. Supporting and Opposing Edwards and the Great Awakening

    A. Because of his support for the Great Awakening, some accused him of enthusiasm, or confusing emotions with real religion.

    B. Edwards responded by writing, *A Treatise Concerning Religious Affections*.

    C. He wrote a treatise on original sin.

        i. B.B. Warfield and John Murray claimed he taught the immediate imputation of Adam's sin—the orthodox Reformed view of Edwards' time.

        ii. Charles Hodge and William Cunningham claimed he taught the mediate imputation of Adam's sin.

        iii. Samuel Baird and John Gerstner claimed he taught neither of those, but a new idea of the identification of the sinner with Adam.

    D. Edwards died in his early fifties after being inoculated against smallpox.

STUDY QUESTIONS

1. _____ was started because Harvard had embraced liberal ideas.
    a. Yale
    b. Princeton
    c. William and Mary
    d. Brown

2. Jonathan Edwards described his conversion as taking place when he was overwhelmed by a sense of the beauty and glory of God in nature.
    a. True
    b. False

3. Edwards's millennial views were strongly _____.
    a. Premillenial
    b. Postmillenial
    c. Amillenial
    d. Panmillenial

4. Edwards taught that the millennium had actually begun in the 1740s.
    a. True
    b. False

5. The reason Edwards was fired from his church was tied to his views on
    _____.

    a. The millennium
    b. Predestination
    c. Church membership
    d. Elder oversight

DISCUSSION QUESTIONS

1. What are some negative ways that the so called "triumph of the laity" has affected
    church life in America?

2. Explain how Edwards saw revivals functioning within God's work in history.
    What does Dr. Godfrey say is a better understanding of how He acts?

3. Edwards, who studied for 12 or 13 hours a day, was disappointed that other
    Christians weren't so disciplined. Read 1 Corinthians 12:12—20 and explain how
    a right understanding of different gifts could prevent such disappointment.

12

Political Revolutions

MESSAGE INTRODUCTION

Coming at the close of the eighteenth century, the American and French Revolutions had an enormous impact on subsequent history. While both movements were revolutionary in nature, you will see how different their aim and character were. In this lecture, Dr. Godfrey will highlight some of the key points of these events, showing especially how the American Revolution affected American church history.

SCRIPTURE READINGS

Romans 13:1–7; 1 Peter 2:13–17

TEACHING OBJECTIVES

1. To see how the Great Awakening affected the political and ecclesiastical history of the United States
2. To explain how the American Revolution affected church life in the United States
3. To show how the American and French Revolutions differed from one another, especially in their approach to Christianity and tradition

QUOTATION

The reason why we ought to be subject to magistrates is, because they are constituted by God's ordination. For since it pleases God thus to govern the world, he who attempts to invert the order of God, and thus to resist God himself, despises his power; since to despise the providence of him who is the founder of civil power, is to carry on war with him. Understand further, that powers are from God, not as pestilence, and famine, and wars, and other visitations for sin, are said to be from him; but because he has appointed them for the legitimate and just government of the world. For though tyrannies and unjust exercise of power, as they are full of disorder, (ἀταξίας) are not an ordained government; yet the right of government is ordained by God for the wellbeing of mankind.

As it is lawful to repel wars and to seek remedies for other evils, hence the Apostle commands us willingly and cheerfully to respect and honor the right and authority of magistrates, as useful to men: for the punishment which God inflicts on men for their sins, we cannot properly call ordinations, but they are the means which he designedly appoints for the preservation of legitimate order.

—John Calvin

LECTURE OUTLINE

I.   From the Great Awakening to the Dawn of the American Revolution

   A.   The US grew dramatically in the eighteenth century.
      i.   In 1713 it had 360,000 people.
      ii.   In 1760 it had 1.6 million.
      iii. In 1776 it had grown to 3 million.

   B.   One of the effects of the Great Awakening was that Americans became more concerned about what was going on in America than what was going on in England.

   C.   In the 1760s, there was rumor that the king was going to send a bishop to America.
      i.   Bishops were part of the aristocracy, and Americans were afraid that England might export its whole aristocratic hierarchy to America.
      ii.   The great fear of "episcopacy" began to rally anti-royal sentiment, especially among Presbyterians and Congregationalists.

   D.   There was a rising sentiment where Americans wanted their rights as Englishmen, and did not want to be taxed without having representation in Parliament.

II. The Leaders of the American Revolution

   A.   They were at least in formal terms Christians.
   B.   They knew that Christians were obliged to honor and obey those in authority over them.
   C.   For many of them, taking up arms against the king was a very serious matter.
   D.   There was a well-established Calvinist political theory that said a monarch can only be opposed if he becomes a tyrant.
   E.   The notion of tyranny was clear—not only do subjects have responsibilities to their rulers, but rulers also have responsibilities to their subjects.
   F.   The Declaration of Independence states that the king has violated his responsibility to his subjects.
   G.   It was a revolution not to tear down, but to maintain traditional rights.

III. Religious Freedom

   A.   This was one of the ideas embedded in the Constitution.
   B.   Most assumed the country would remain Protestant.
   C.   The point was that there wouldn't be federal legislation making everyone Anglican, Presbyterian, etc.

    D. Such religious freedom meant the separation of the church and state on the federal level.

    E. It was a key contributing factor to the notion of denominationalism.
       i. The heart of denominationalism is that one denomination before the law is just as good as another.
      ii. The attitude of denominations is that differences are taken seriously, but such differences don't divide from God.

IV. The Disestablishment of the Church

    A. Disestablishment meant that the church received no tax money.

    B. Whatever the church did, the laity had to pay for.

    C. This led to a spirit of volunteerism.

V. The French Revolution

    A. The French Revolution was driven much more by a conviction that traditions needed to be torn down.

    B. There was a progressive radicalization of the French Revolution.

    C. It began in 1789.
       i. King Louis XVI called the Estates General into session to get their support for reform.
      ii. The Estates General radicalized itself within a couple months and reconstituted itself as a national assembly with real parliamentary powers.
      iii. They limited the power of the King.
      iv. They confiscated church property.
        – The Roman Catholic Church owned about twenty percent of all the property in France.

    D. In 1791, freedom of religion was declared for all.

    E. In 1792, France was declared a republic, and the king and queen were executed soon thereafter.

    F. 1793 and 1794 saw the "reign of terror" in which anyone sympathetic to the royalist cause was beheaded by the guillotine.

    G. They even experimented with a ten-day workweek.

    H. Relative peace was established in 1799, and then Napoleon Bonaparte took control.

STUDY QUESTIONS

1. In the 1760s, rumors began to circulate that the King of England was thinking about sending a(n) _____ to America.
    a. Advisor
    b. Bishop
    c. Commander
    d. Duke

2. One of the effects of the Great Awakening was that Americans shifted their attention from England to America itself.
   a. True
   b. False

3. The disestablishment of the church meant that it received no _____ from the government.
   a. Tax money
   b. Special privileges
   c. Official recognition
   d. Religious protection

4. The American Revolution was a revolution to maintain traditional rights.
   a. True
   b. False

5. The period during the French Revolution when anyone sympathetic to the royalist cause was put to death is known as the _____.
   a. Rule of the thirty tyrants
   b. Reign of terror
   c. Dominion of Robespierre
   d. Supremacy of the Republic

BIBLE STUDY AND DISCUSSION QUESTIONS

1. Explain the well-established Calvinist political theory that many Americans saw as support for opposing the monarchy.

2. How did the disestablishment of the church lead to the so-called "triumph of the laity"?

3. What are the similarities and differences between the American and French Revolutions?